1/07

KURT BUSCH

JANEY LEVY

HIGH
interest
books

Children's Press®
A Division of Scholastic Inc.
New York / Toronto / London / Auckland / Sydney
Mexico City / New Delhi / Hong Kong
Danbury, Connecticut

Book Design: Dean Galiano
Contributing Editor: Geeta Sobha
Photo Credits: Cover © Streeter Lecka/Getty Images for NASCAR; pg. 4 © Tom
Copeland/Allsport/Getty Images; pg. 7 © Robert Laberge/Allsport/Getty Images; pg. 10 ©
Jamie Squire/Getty Images for NASCAR; pg. 12 Getty Images for NASCAR; pg. 13 © Todd
Warshaw/Getty Images for NASCAR; pg. 14 © Tim Boyd/AP Photo; pg. 18 © Jonathan
Ferrey/Getty Images; pgs. 20, 22, 39 © Rusty Jarrett/Getty Images; pg. 24 © Mike
McCarn/AP Photo; pg. 28 © Darrell Ingham/Getty Images; pg. 30 © Tracy T. Mendez, Daily
Journal/AP Photo; pg. 32 Icon SMI/Corbis; pg. 36 Getty Images for NASCAR; pg. 38 ©
Chris Graythen/Getty Images

Library of Congress Cataloging-in-Publication Data

Levy, Janey.
    Kurt Busch / Janey Levy.
    p. cm. — (Stock car racing)
    Includes index.
    ISBN-10: 0-531-16806-9 (lib. bdg.)   0-531-18714-4 (pbk.)
    ISBN-13: 978-0-531-16806-6 (lib. bdg.)   978-0-531-18714-2 (pbk.)
    1. Busch, Kurt, 1978—Juvenile literature. 2. Automobile racing drivers—
United States—Biography—Juvenile literature. 3. Stock car racing—United
States—Juvenile literature. I. Title. II. Series.

GV1032.B89L48 2007
796.72092-dc22

                                                    2006007596

TABLE OF CONTENTS

Introduction   5
1 Growing Up
      on the Fast Track   8
2 Rising Star   16
3 Rough Road   26
4 Life Away From
      the Track   34
New Words   42
For Further
      Reading   44
Resources   45
Index   47
About the Author   48

Kurt is geared up for a practice run at the Bristol Motor Speedway in Tennessee.

INTRODUCTION

You're racing your car near the front of the pack on one of the short tracks you really like to drive. Suddenly there is an accident ahead. You hit your breaks immediately as the caution flag is waved to slow down the drivers. At this time, your crew chief wants you to make a pit stop to get new tires. Your tires are worn and probably will not last until the end of the race. You can take the lead, however, if you stay out on the track. You make a split-second decision and ignore your crew chief. You keep racing. As the drivers pick up speed again, you make your move—and take the lead! Seconds later, you zip across the finish line. The roar of the crowd tells you that you have won another big race!

This may sound more like the stuff of books and movies than real life. However, it really happened to Kurt Busch in the Food City 500 race at Bristol Motor Speedway in 2004. That win marked the start of a very good year for Kurt. He went on to win the National Association for Stock Car Auto Racing (NASCAR) top honor, the Nextel Cup Championship.

In just a few years, Kurt has become one of the best-known names in auto racing. In fact, Kurt has become one of the top names in all of sports! His love of racing began at an early age-and for a good reason. His father, Tom, used to race cars, and he obviously passed on his love of the sport to Kurt.

From his early days behind the wheel of a go-kart to his enormous worldwide popularity as a NASCAR superstar, Kurt Busch has been on the fast track of success-and his career has been as exciting as any car race he's won.

How did Kurt get started? What has racing taught him? What challenges has Kurt faced in his rise to the top of his field? Let's find out more about his racing background and how racing has changed Kurt's life.

At a pit stop, Kurt's crew works quickly changing tires, filling the gas tank, and making any necessary repairs.

CHAPTER ONE

GROWING UP ON THE FAST TRACK

Kurt was only twenty-six years old when he won the Nextel Cup Championship. Most race car drivers are just starting their careers at that age. Kurt had already been racing for twelve years. His connection to the world of racing goes back even further than that. Kurt grew up around racetracks. Under the guidance of his father, he has become one of today's top race car drivers.

FAMILY TIES

Kurt was born in Las Vegas, Nevada, on August 4, 1978. Kurt's parents are Tom and Gaye Busch. Cars and racing always played an important role in Busch family life. Tom was an auto mechanic and auto parts salesman. He was active in the local stock car racing scene. Tom was not a big-time race car driver. However, he won about one hundred races and several championships at local speedways.

Kurt was a member of his father's racing crew by the time he was a teenager. His younger brother, Kyle, also helped out when he was old enough. Kurt and Kyle learned a lot about cars and racing from their father.

GROOMED FOR SUCCESS

Tom taught his sons all about racing. He believes that a good racer needs to know everything about cars. He made sure Kurt and Kyle knew how to build a car from scratch. The boys learned all about the special parts that a race car needs.

Tom also wanted Kurt and Kyle to know how to prepare for a race. They would need to understand the special features of each racetrack. They needed to

Winning the Nextel Cup trophy is the goal for all NASCAR drivers. Kurt's parents, Tom and Gaye, are proud that Kurt has achieved this goal at such a young age.

understand the other drivers, too. Tom even taught his sons how to manage a racing team.

KURT'S EARLY RACES

Kurt took his father's lessons to heart. He started out racing go-karts when he was only fourteen years old. These tiny vehicles can race at speeds greater than 100 miles (161 kilometers) per hour. Racing go-karts helps drivers develop many of the skills needed to race larger vehicles. Drivers also learn how to control their vehicles with precision, how to make split-second decisions, and how to react quickly. Many race car drivers have started out racing go-karts.

Kurt moved up to dwarf cars just two years later. His talent in driving these small cars was apparent right away. Kurt was named the Nevada Rookie of the Year in dwarf car racing in 1994. He won the Nevada State Dwarf Car Championship the very next year.

FAST FACT

Kurt's dad, Tom, won the Nevada Dwarf Car Championship in 1994. That's the same year Kurt won Rookie of the Year in dwarf car racing.

Go-karts were created in the 1950s. Young drivers use go-karts to practice racing before moving on to bigger vehicles.

Kurt continued to develop his racing skills over the next few years. He raced in several classes and won many honors. In 1996, he won a championship in a class of cars known as hobby stock cars. He was also named Rookie of the Year in a class of small cars

12

KURT'S YOUNGER BROTHER

Kurt's younger brother, Kyle, is also a NASCAR driver. Kyle started racing when he was thirteen years old. Kyle had won two championships and more than sixty-five races by the time he was sixteen. He joined the NASCAR team operated by Hendrick Motorsports in 2003. He started out racing in the Busch Series, which is NASCAR's second largest racing series sponsored by Anheuser-Busch, Inc. Then Hendrick Motorsports moved Kyle up to the Nextel Cup Series in 2005. Kyle scored a success in the second race of the season. He became the youngest Nextel Cup driver ever to earn the right to start the race in the first position, which is called the pole position.

known as legend cars. In 1997, Kurt ran a few races in a special type of stock car known as a featherlite. He completed his first full year in the Featherlite Southwest Series in 1998. Once again, he did so well that he was named Rookie of the Year. In 1999, he became the youngest Featherlite Southwest Series champion ever! That year marked a turning point in Kurt's career.

The Featherlite Modified Series' rules differ from other NASCAR racing series. Cars are lower and have softer tires.

Roush Racing offered Kurt the chance to try out for a job as a driver with their truck team in the Craftsman Truck Series. Roush Racing is one of the biggest organizations in NASCAR racing. This is the kind of opportunity every young driver dreams about.

In the fall of 1999, Kurt drove two tests for Roush Racing. He has said that he was more nervous during these tests than he had ever been before. He did not do well in the first test. He did very well, however, in the second test. Roush Racing offered him the job. Kurt was now driving in the big leagues—and he was only twenty-one years old!

CHAPTER TWO

RISING STAR

When Kurt joined Roush Racing, he was to drive the Number 99 truck, a Ford F-150. He ran his first race in the Craftsman Truck Series in February 2000 and came in second. Kurt was off to a great start.

Kurt went on to win four races in that year's Craftsman Truck Series. He came in second four times. He had thirteen top-five finishes and seventeen top-ten finishes. He won the pole position four times. Kurt finished the season in second place in the points standings. Drivers earn points for how well they do in each race. The driver with the most points at the end of the year wins the championship. Kurt did not win the championship, but he came close. It was a spectacular first year. He easily won the Rookie of the Year award.

NASCAR'S TOP LEVEL

Jack Roush, the head of Roush Racing, was so impressed with Kurt that he made an extraordinary decision. In 2001, he decided to move Kurt to NASCAR's top level of racing. This was known at the time as the Winston Cup Series; it is now called the Nextel Cup Series. Kurt was going to drive in the top-level series after only one year in the Craftsman Truck Series. Most young drivers spend a few years developing their skills in the Craftsman Truck Series. Then they spend a few years in the Busch Series. Roush, however, believed that Kurt was talented enough to go straight to the Winston Cup Series. Kurt actually drove in seven Winston Cup races at the end of the 2000 season. He did not do especially well in any of these races. Instead, he gained valuable experience.

NASCAR's Craftsman Truck Series features vehicles that look like pick-up trucks. These automobiles, however, are racing machines that can reach up to 190 miles (306 kilometers) per hour.

THE POLE POSITION

Vehicles line up in rows to start a race. The positions in these rows are determined by how fast drivers go during qualifying runs. In qualifying, each driver individually runs a few laps around the track as fast as he or she can go. The one who goes the fastest gets to start the race on the front row in the inside spot. This is known as the pole position. The term "pole position" has been carried over to car racing from horse racing. In horse racing, there are a series of poles along the inside of the track.

Kurt's first full year at this racing level was 2001. He enjoyed some successes in spite of his youth and lack of experience in the big leagues. He drove the Number 97 Ford Taurus. He won the pole position in the Southern 500 race at Darlington Raceway, which is considered NASCAR's toughest superspeedway. Altogether, Kurt had three top-five finishes and six top-ten finishes for the season. He was also runner-up for Rookie of the Year.

Kurt had a good rookie year. Still, he finished the season in twenty-seventh place in the points standings. Jack Roush thought Kurt had the talent to do much better than that. He believed Kurt could improve if he worked with a different crew. So Roush switched the crews of Kurt's Number 97 car and Mark Martin's Number 6 car.

At the Dodge Charger 500, on May 7, 2005, Kurt hits a wall in the second lap. He finished the race at thirty-seventh place.

WINNING WITH FENNIG

Kurt started 2002 with a new crew and a new crew chief named Jimmy Fennig. Fennig is a highly respected crew chief who has been in racing for more than thirty years. He has worked with many of NASCAR's top drivers. Fennig started out as a racer on dirt tracks and then became a mechanic for other racers. He worked his way up over the years to become a crew chief. In 2002, Kurt's was one of the best second-year performances ever in NASCAR. He gave a lot of the credit to Fennig. Kurt had his first NASCAR win that year in the Food City 500 race at Bristol Motor Speedway. He went on to win three more races. He won the pole position once. He also had twelve top-five finishes and twenty-one top-ten finishes. Kurt finished the season in third place in the points standings. This was an amazing accomplishment for such a young driver.

WINNING WAYS

Though Kurt's hopes were high at the beginning of the 2003 season, he finished the season eleventh in the points standings. Kurt won four races again, but he had fewer top-five and top-ten finishes.

A NASCAR championship is the result of a team effort. Here, crew chief Jimmy Fennig talks to Kurt at the 2004 Nextel Cup Championship.

In 2004, Kurt had the kind of year every driver dreams about. This was the year that the sponsorship of the series changed and the Winston Cup Series became the Nextel Cup Series. It was also the first year that NASCAR had a Chase for the Championship playoff at the end of the season. The ten drivers who had the most points would take part in the playoff.

Kurt did very well in the first part of the 2004 season. Then his performance began to drop. Kurt and his crew became concerned that he might not earn a spot in the playoff. Fennig and the crew found a way to improve the setup on the Number 97 car. The setup involves planning pit stops, repairs, or tire changes during the race to allow for the best time. With these changes, Kurt landed a spot in the playoff.

Altogether, Kurt won one pole position and three races in 2004. He also had ten top-five finishes and twenty-one top-ten finishes. He earned a lot of bonus points for the number of laps he led in different races. Kurt did extremely well in the playoff and won the Nextel Cup Championship. He was only twenty-six years old.

Though these successes make Kurt's NASCAR career seem like a fairy tale, there were problems along the way.

Many of the difficulties were of Kurt's own making. He is an aggressive driver who has crumpled more than a few fenders. His behavior toward his crew, other racers, and NASCAR officials has been very offensive at times.

FAST FACT

Successful crew chief Jimmy Fennig has high praise for Kurt. "He is unbelievable. He makes our job easier because he has so much talent. He can get up on that wheel and drive the wheels off a car!"

Team owner Jack Roush discusses strategy with Kurt Busch during the 2004 Nextel Cup series. It was Roush Racing's second top-level championship.

CHAPTER THREE

ROUGH ROAD

It can be easy to forget that racing is a team sport. The driver is the most visible member of the team and gets the most attention. Without a good crew and crew chief to keep the car running in peak condition, however, even the best driver can fail. The driver and the crew need to work well together and treat each other with respect. Kurt took a while to learn how to work with his crew.

Kurt likes things to run perfectly. At first, he was quick to get angry and criticize members of the crew when something went wrong. This approach caused bad feelings. Kurt had to learn to voice his feelings professionally and maturely. Learning how to do this took time.

Kurt's bold driving style has annoyed many drivers he has raced against. He is quite willing to bump other drivers to get them out of his way. He does not care if the driver is young, like himself, or a veteran. This has angered many veteran drivers. They feel that Kurt is not showing them the respect he should. Some people have called him arrogant. Others have described him as a spoiled brat.

BUSCH VERSUS SPENCER

Kurt's driving style and attitude caused even bigger problems with veteran driver Jimmy Spencer. An all-out feud erupted. The problems between Kurt and Spencer started in 2001. Kurt claimed Spencer had knocked him out of a race at the Phoenix International Speedway. Kurt got back at Spencer in a race a few months later. The two drivers were battling for the lead in the Food City 500 at Bristol Motor

Speedway in early 2002. Kurt took the lead and won the race by bumping Spencer out of his way. This made Spencer angry. He promised he would not forget what Kurt had done to him.

Here, Kurt and Jimmy Spencer duke it out side by side at the NASCAR Winston Cup Banquet 400 on October 5, 2003.

Spencer crashed into Kurt in the Brickyard 400 at the Indianapolis Motor Speedway later in 2002. Spencer was able to keep racing after the crash. Kurt's car, however, was so damaged that he had to quit the race. Kurt got very angry and said some nasty things about Spencer. NASCAR officials thought the feud between the two drivers had gone on long enough. They ordered Kurt and Spencer to cool it, but that was not the end of the feud.

In 2003, Kurt bumped into Spencer in a race at Michigan International Speedway. He was hoping to knock Spencer out of the race. He did not succeed, but Spencer was very upset. Kurt went on to win the race. Spencer was so angry that he bumped Kurt's car after the race was over. Then Spencer got out of his car and punched Kurt in the face. NASCAR officials had had enough. They fined both drivers and placed them on probation for the rest of the season.

ANGER MANAGEMENT

Kurt's behavior also made him unpopular with many fans. They knew he was a great driver, but they did not like his behavior. Kurt knew he had to improve his image. He tried to learn to control his temper. He made efforts to deal with problems in a mature way. He seemed to be making progress, but it has not always been easy.

Kurt shows his anger to driver Jimmy Spencer after the crash at the Brickyard 400, that forced Kurt out of the race.

Kurt's temper has even affected his dealings with NASCAR officials. During one race at Darlington in 2005, Kurt was angry about official instructions after an accident. He said some offensive words over his car radio. He also threw a water bottle when he got back to his pit stall on pit road. The bottle hit a NASCAR official.

Another incident in 2005 involved the crew of driver Scott Riggs. Riggs crashed into Kurt at the New Hampshire International Speedway. The crash occurred because Riggs lost control of his car. Kurt's car was damaged so he had to quit the race. He was so angry that he went to Riggs's pit stall to speak with the crew chief. This is against NASCAR rules, which do not allow drivers to enter each other's pit areas.

Then a sheriff's deputy stopped Kurt for driving recklessly and running a stop sign in November 2005. It happened near Phoenix, Arizona. The deputy at first thought Kurt was drunk, but that proved not to be true. Kurt argued with the deputy and said disrespectful things to him. In the end, Kurt was charged with reckless driving.

Kurt publicly apologized for his behavior the next day, but the damage had been done. Jack Roush

31

decided that Kurt's bad behavior had finally gone too far. Roush publicly criticized Kurt. He suspended Kurt for the last two races of the season.

Kurt had already made plans to leave Roush Racing after the 2006 season. He had signed a contract to join Penske Racing in 2007. Now everyone decided it would be best for Kurt to leave Roush Racing early. So Kurt joined Penske Racing a year early to drive the Number 2 car, a Dodge Charger.

Kurt loses control of his car and crashes after being hit by Scott Riggs. The action took place at the New Hampshire International Speedway.

CHAPTER FOUR

LIFE AWAY FROM THE TRACK

There is also another side to Kurt. Off the racetrack he is a different person. People who know Kurt personally say he is just a normal guy. The self-important, aggressive young driver with a temper almost seems to disappear when Kurt is away from the racetrack. He is relaxed and quiet, almost shy. He tells funny stories, sometimes about himself. Kurt has many fun hobbies that he enjoys, such as listening to music. His favorite band is Aerosmith.

AWAY FROM THE TRACKS

One of the things Kurt does regularly is exercise. Racers have to be in excellent physical condition. Controlling a heavy car as it speeds around a racetrack is hard work. Kurt likes to do cardiovascular workouts to keep his heart and blood vessels strong and healthy.

Kurt also likes to spend time watching sports. He is a huge baseball fan and enjoys attending baseball games. He also likes to visit different baseball parks around the country. Kurt's favorite team is the Chicago Cubs. This may be because of his family background—both his parents are originally from Chicago. Kurt also likes to relax by playing golf.

Not surprisingly, Kurt also enjoys playing video racing games. He started playing them as a boy and still plays them. As you might expect, he's very good. He won the NASCAR 500 video game tournament in 2003.

GIVING BACK

Some of Kurt's time away from the racetrack is spent doing charity work. Kurt became involved with

Rebuilding Together during his time with Roush Racing. Rebuilding Together works to make sure that low-income homeowners have a clean, safe place to live. Rebuilding Together provides necessary repairs to

In July 2005, Kurt takes part in the Racin' the Bases Celebrity Softball Game. This charity benefits a camp for children with life-threatening diseases.

homeowners' houses free of charge. Kurt has even helped make some of those repairs.

FAMILY AND FRIENDS

Kurt got his own new home in 2003. He bought a farm right outside Mooresville, North Carolina. He enjoys riding his tractor around the farm, and he even has two goats there.

Family plays an important role in Kurt's time away from the track. He moved his whole family to his North Carolina farm. Mom, Dad, Grandma, and brother Kyle all live there.

Kurt's family now has someone new: Eva. Kurt and Eva met on a blind date in 2003. The friend who arranged the date told Eva that Kurt was a veterinarian. It turned out that Eva liked Kurt and did not mind that he was a racer. The couple became engaged in 2005.

FAST FACT

Kurt attended the University of Arizona for one year before he got serious about his racing career. He was planning to be a pharmacist.

Kurt celebrates his win at the Food City 500 on March 26, 2006.

RACING ON

So what does the future hold for Kurt? Of course, no one can say for sure. The past, however, suggests that whatever happens will be exciting. Now as a driver with Penske, he is certain to give us a wild ride on the fast track. Kurt is definitely a driver to keep an eye on.

After the Food City 500 race, Kurt shows off his trophy.

KURT BUSCH TIMELINE

August 4, 1978	Born in Las Vegas, Nevada
1992	Begins racing go-karts
1994	Begins racing dwarf cars; wins Nevada Rookie of the Year
1995	Wins Nevada Dwarf Car Championship
1996	Hobby Stock champion at the Bullring at the Las Vegas Motor Speedway; Legend Car National Rookie of the Year
1998	Featherlite Southwest Series Rookie of the Year
1999	Youngest Featherlite Southwest Series champion; wins a ride with Roush Racing's truck team in Craftsman Truck Series
2000	Second in the final points standings in Craftsman Truck Series; Rookie of the Year
2001	Begins racing in Nextel Cup Series (then called Winston Cup series); wins his first pole position; has three top-five finishes and six top-ten finishes

Wins first Winston Cup race; wins a total of four Winston Cup races for the season; has twelve top-five finishes and twenty-one top-ten finishes; is third in points standings at the end of the season

Wins four races; has nine top-five finishes and fourteen top-ten finishes; wins no pole positions; is eleventh in points standings at the end of the season; moves his entire family to a farm he purchases in North Carolina; meets his future wife

Wins three races; has ten top-five finishes and twenty-one top-ten finishes; wins Nextel Cup Championship

Wins three races; has six top-five finishes and fifteen top-ten finishes; wins no pole positions; suspended for last two races of the season after being charged with reckless driving near Phoenix, Arizona; leaves Roush Racing

Joins Penske Racing

NEW WORDS

cardiovascular (**kar**-dee-oh-**vas**-kyuh-luhr) having to do with the heart and blood vessels

class (**klass**) a group or set that shares common features

crew chief (**kroo cheef**) the person in charge of the crew of people who work on a race car

pit road (**pit rohd**) the area next to the racetrack where crews work on the cars during a race

pit stall (**pit stawl**) the area on the pit road assigned to a team to use during pit stops

pit stop (**pit stop**) a stop at a pit stall during a race so that the crew can add fuel to the car, change the tires, or make repairs

probation (proh-**bay**-shuhn) a period of time for testing a person's behavior or job qualifications

racetrack (**rayss**-trak) a round or oval course that is used for racing

NEW WORDS

ride (**ride**) a job as a driver on a racing team

rookie (**ruk**-ee) someone who is in their first season in a major professional sport

setup (**set**-uhp) the tuning and adjustments made to a car before and during a race

short track (**short trak**) a racetrack that is less than 1 mile (1.6 km) in length

speedway (**speed**-way) a racetrack for cars

stock car (**stok kar**) a race car built to look like an ordinary car

strategy (**strat**-uh-jee) a clever plan for achieving a goal

suspend (suh-**spend**) to punish someone by stopping the person from taking part in an activity for a short while

FOR FURTHER READING

Buckley, James. *NASCAR*. New York: DK Children's
  Publishing, 2005.

Cavin, Curt. *Under the Helmet: Inside the Mind of a Driver*.
  Chanhassen, MN: Child's World, 2003.

Kelley, K. C., and Bob Woods. *Young Stars of NASCAR*.
  Pleasantville, NY: Reader's Digest Children's
  Publishing, 2005.

Stevens, Josh. *Kurt Busch*. St. Louis, MO: Reedy Press, 2005.

Woods, Bob. *Earning a Ride: How to Become a NASCAR
  Driver*. Chanhassen, MN: Child's World, 2003.

Woods, Bob. *The Greatest Races*. Pleasantville, NY: Reader's
  Digest Children's Publishing, 2004.

RESOURCES

ORGANIZATIONS

ASA Racing
457 South Ridgewood Ave., Suite 101
Daytona Beach, FL 32114
Phone: (386) 258-2221
Fax: (386) 258-2226
http://www.asa-racing.com

National Association for Stock Car Auto Racing
(NASCAR)
1801 W. International Speedway Blvd.
Daytona Beach, FL 32115
Phone: (386) 253-0611
www.nascar.com

USAC National Office
4910 W. 16th St.
Speedway, IN 46224
Phone: (317) 247-5151
www.usacracing.com

RESOURCES

WEB SITES

American Speed Association
www.asa-racing.com
This colorful Web site features the latest news from the American Speed Association (ASA), a stock car racing organization that specializes in oval track racing in the Midwest.

NASCAR
www.nascar.com
Check out the official Web site of NASCAR for up-to-the-minute coverage of news, statistics and information on races, drivers, teams, and industry events.

Penske Racing
www.penskeracing.com
This informative site features a complete Kurt Busch biography, photos, and histories of Penske and NASCAR and Penske and the Indianapolis 500.

INDEX

B
Bristol Motor Speedway, 21

C
cardiovascular, 35
class, 12, 14
Craftsman Truck Series, 16-18, 40
crew chief, 5, 21

D
Darlington Raceway, 19
dwarf car, 11-12, 40

F
Featherlite cars, 15, 40
Fennig, Jimmy, 21-22
Food City 500, 6, 21, 27, 38-39

G
go-kart, 11-12, 40

I
Indianapolis Motor Speedway, 29

N
Nextel Cup Championship, 6, 8,
    22–23, 41
Nextel Cup Series, 13, 17, 23, 25,
    40

P
Penske Racing, 33, 38, 41
Phoenix International Speedway, 27
pit road, 31
pit stall, 31
pit stop, 5, 23
probation, 29

R
racetrack, 8-9, 34-35
ride, 38, 40
Riggs, Scott, 31

INDEX

rookie, 11, 14, 17, 19, 40
Roush Racing, 15-17, 33, 40

S
setup, 23
short track, 5
speedway, 6, 9, 21, 27-29, 31, 40
Spencer, Jimmy, 27-30
stock car, 6, 9, 14
strategy, 25
suspension, 33, 41

T
temper, 30-31, 34
tires, 5

W
Winston Cup Series, 17, 23, 28, 40-41

ABOUT THE AUTHOR

Janey Levy is a writer and editor who lives in Colden, New York. She is the author of more than fifty books for young people.